ROBERT DAVID MacDONALD

THE ICE HOUSE

Oberon Books
London

First published in 1998 by Oberon Books Ltd
(incorporating Absolute Classics),
521 Caledonian Road, London N7 9RH.
Tel: 0171 607 3637 / Fax: 0171 607 3629

British Library Cataloguing-in-Publication Data

A catalogue record for this book is available from the British Library.

ISBN 1 84002 030 X

Cover design: Andrzej Klimowski

Typography: Richard Doust

Printed in Great Britain by Arrowhead Books, Reading.

THE ICE HOUSE

CHARACTERS

BRYAN: – forty-something, a writer

HELIER: – thirty-something, a writer

ROD: – twenty-something

The setting is the living-room in BRYAN and HELIER's apartment on the top floor of an expensive block in a large city. One wall is mostly given up to a picture window, with a view down over a park. There are two doors, one leading to the hall and kitchen, the other to the bedrooms and bathrooms. Prominent is a drinks trolley or cabinet.

The Ice House was first performed at the Citizens' Theatre Glasgow on the 7th January 1998. It was directed by Robert David MacDonald with the following cast:

BRYAN, *Derwent Watson*

HELIER, *Andrea Hart*

ROD, *Henry Ian Cusick*

Designer, *Kenny Miller*

Lighting designer, *Paul Sorley*

But, Cupid, now farewell, I will go play me
With thoughts that please me less, but less betray me.

FULKE GREVILLE

Scene One

Mid-morning. Winter. HELIER still in her dressing gown, staring out of the window. BRYAN mixing a drink at the trolley.

BRYAN: Ice? Where?

HELIER: Where it always is. Do you really want – need a drink at this hour?

BRYAN: Yes.

HELIER: Fine.

BRYAN: Doesn't sound it.

HELIER: Don't suppose it does.

BRYAN: You think everyone who wants a drink is a drunk?

HELIER: No, but I *know* that everyone who is a drunk wants a drink.

She picks up a dictation pad.

Don't you think we should try and get on? No, I won't make you a present of that one. Shall we continue?

BRYAN: Where did we leave things? Unambiguous enough for you?

HELIER: Even me.

Reads back her shorthand

"As a matter of principle ..." Now that could be the start of just about any single paragraph you've ever written. God, I wish you'd get a proper secretary.

BRYAN: No more fervently than I. However, since
you are barely able to boil a kettle, much less an
egg, and since a succession of sullen domestics,
reduced to mutinous inefficiency by your total lack
of consideration for them, obviate the need for you
ever to wield as much as a mop in your own defence,
while your chronic intemperance renders you
incapable, after a certain hour, of cultivated human
communication, social, mental, moral or while we're
at it sexual, is it too much to ask you to employ the
faint skill acquired in your search for a living, or
putting it plainer a husband, namely your shorthand,
only marginally easier to decode than your longhand,
to ease that husband's professional path? In other
words, Frau Pitman's Improv-éd, shift your fat arse.
What principle was it this time, and where, finally,
is the ice?

HELIER: In the kitchen, assuming, perhaps recklessly,
that you, or even I remembered to refill the trays
idle slattern oh shit I'll go. Pour me something while
you're waiting? If you're under starter's orders,
I might as well keep pace, or track at least.

*Goes and returns quickly with ice-bucket while BRYAN
mixes a Martini.*

Under your very nose. Mix that properly and
I promise I won't kiss you – not even try.

BRYAN hands her a glass.

Thank you. So what principle?

Back to shorthand.

"As a matter of principle, there is no room for
enjoyment in conceptual art. The artists concerned
know how to remove this ideological gangrene, by
cutting off desire ..."

BRYAN: Just a minute. Insert "because desire is always feudal ..."

HELIER: (*Brightly acidic, an intentionally audible aside.*) Why, so it is.

BRYAN: "The work then is no longer formal, but simply visual, articulating merely a perception and a nomination ..."

HELIER: (*As before.*) Speak for yourself. Nothing mere about my perceptions thank you.

BRYAN: "With desire ruled out" – and do stop interrupting all the time – "With desire ruled out, discourse returns to strength. Art turns talkative when it stops being erotic."

HELIER: (*As before.*) To whom do you tell it?

BRYAN: "The limits of Art may have been pushed back, but the price to pay is a stiff one. Nothing less than the abandoning of those pleasures that crystallise around the dark erections of the mind ..."

HELIER: (*Wide awake.*) Do you mean that? Dark erections? Forsooth! Bryan, are we mapping out new territories?

BRYAN: No such luck. Alright then – "But the price to pay – dash – and the exorbitancy of the price is determined by the individual psychology – dash – is aphanasis."

HELIER: It's what?

BRYAB: A. P. H. A. ... You think I ought to explain? Oh, well, "loss of desire, castration ..."

HELIER: Now I can die happy.

BRYAN: Don't bother.

HELIER: (*As her pencil point breaks.*) Bloody thing. Is there much more of this?

BRYAN: End of a chapter. More or less. As for anything else – absolutely nothing. And not long now to do it in.

HELIER: (*Helpful.*) Dig something out of a drawer?

BRYAN: Take longer to cobble it together than starting over properly.

HELIER: You need someone to file things for you. Other than your nails. And no I won't.

BRYAN: Well you may be – *will* be pleased to hear all that is a thing of the past. I am I hope seeing a boy today.

HELIER: Would I could say the same. In your case that doesn't inevitably signal a reduction in paperwork, just work.

BRYAN: He comes highly recommended.

HELIER: By?

BRYAN: Courtney Newnham. Even you can hardly quibble about that. Take a look.

He hands her a letter.

HELIER: (*Reading it.*) Can he be this good?

BRYAN: Like writing your own reviews.

HELIER: Goodness, Courtney's handwriting's a bit adrift, isn't it? Looks like it was done on a merry-go-round.

BRYAN: That I doubt. But he has been ill.

HELIER: We must get in touch with him. We've hardly seen him since Marjorie died.

BRYAN: I'll ring him over the weekend: about the reference. You can't complain about it, can you?

HELIER: And shan't. When does this paragon arrive?

BRYAN: He should be here. The traffic held him up perhaps.

HELIER: I must say you're rather springing it on me. I mean where will he live, do we cater for him at meals, will he want to use the parking space, maybe he has a bicycle, is he a vegetarian, will he need an office of his own, if so where, the spare room I suppose...

BRYAN: We're not adopting him. For all I know he drives a Bentley and lives in guilty splendour in Park West, or alternatively, in poor but honest sordour, if there is such a word, with his mother, a woman as worthy as she is white-haired, in I know not what grim suburb – anyway I am paying him, should he prove what a thoroughly irritating employer would require, a sufficient and regular wage, plus his national insurance, all of which will force me to take advantage of him...

HELIER barks a laugh.

... or at any rate set him to honest but profitable toil between the hours of nine and five, after which he will doubtless disappear, leaving us to our own overblown devices and desires, and that will be very much that.

HELIER: How much of all that do you believe?

BRYAN: Most of it. Most of it.

HELIER: Oh for your touching faith. Just as long as you're really not adopting him. Or something to that effect.

BRYAN: As if.

HELIER: (*Sudden flare-up.*) Oh, do whatever you fucking want.

Long pause. The house telephone rings.

BRYAN: Yes! Oh yes, good morning... No, not late at all... Of course it doesn't matter. Glad you found your way... Come up – the lift's just to your right – we're on the top floor – number fourteen... See you in half a minute.

HELIER: Judging from the tone of wistful charm, that was Tippy the Wonder Scribe, the boy that put the olive into Olivetti.

BRYAN: Yes. The traffic held him up. As I said.

HELIER: I need another drink to hold *me* up. (*Warding him off.*) Not for you.

BRYAN: I'm not a child.

HELIER: I hope he isn't either.

BRYAN: Haven't you got things to do? Reform the postal system, reinvent the brassiere, I don't know.

HELIER: Well, not really, but I ought to change.

BRYAN: Yes, oh, yes. Please yes.

Bell rings.

Go on, bugger off now. I'll answer it.

He goes out.

She does a quick refill of her glass and leaves just as the others re-enter.

Come in, come in, Mr Leonard. Let me take your things. I'm sorry about the traffic: it's always Hell round about midday. Anyway, I'm glad you managed to find the way, not always easy the first time but perhaps you did map-reading in the scouts?

ROD: There always seemed better ways of topping-up one's education.

BRYAN: Of that I have little doubt. Courtney Newnham wrote to me about you – with enthusiasm, I will say.

ROD: I'm glad. He was a remarkable employer.

BRYAN: Why did you leave?

ROD: I became unnecessary.

BRYAN: Surplus to requirements?

ROD: You could put it like that.

BRYAN: I thought I just did.

ROD: Yes.

BRYAN swerves over to the drinks table, finds the shaker empty, and rather frantically mixes some more.

BRYAN: I'm so sorry. I should have offered you one before. I don't know where my manners are. Work has been just piling up of late, but you will change all that won't you? Ice?

ROD: Thank you, I don't drink.

BRYAN: Oh, well, a coke, orange juice, whatever?

ROD: No thank you, really. Nothing for me.

BRYAN: You won't mind then, if I have one?

ROD: No, please, Sir Courtney always used to have a sherry before lunch. Amontillado. Harvey's. Before his stroke, of course.

BRYAN: You're quite sure you won't join me?

ROD: Quite.

BRYAN: Well, then. I hope we shall see eye to eye (*Drinks.*) on most things.

ROD: I see no reason why not.

BRYAN: No.

Gestures him to a chair. ROD takes a different one.

(*Pause.*) There isn't an awful lot to do really – it's just that I like what there is, to be done accurately, filing, classifying and so forth. I'm working on a rather irritating commission at the moment for a popular series, so-called: a sort of prat's guide to aesthetics. I have it all, well most of it, planned – there's just rather a lot of boring hackwork, checking references, getting people's permission for photographs etcetera. I imagine you would be quite up to that, no?

ROD: I would think well up to it.

BRYAN: Yes, I thought as much. Are you sure you won't have something to drink? Lunch may be a while yet.

ROD: No, really, thank you.

BRYAN: Suit yourself.

ROD: That is what I was doing.

BRYAN: My wife should be here any second. She's changing – into what I couldn't say. There are Third World countries spend less on grain than she does on clothes. (*The joke falls flat.*) I can't think what women find to do.

ROD: Really?

BRYAN: (*Irritated by his tone.*) Well, yes, I suppose we can all find something to do for any given occasion, it's just that I... never mind it doesn't matter a bit: does it,

Mr Leonard? Do you have another name? I mean a first name, dare I say Christian? People fling them around nowadays like bread rolls at a bump supper, I know, but it is a useful short cut in relationships – no one has time any more alas for that leisurely schoolboy progress to intimacy from one name to another. (*A self-indulgent sigh.*)

ROD: Rot.

BRYAN: What did you say?

ROD: My name. Rod.

BRYAN: Short for something?

ROD: Not necessarily.

BRYAN: Rodney – Roderick...?

ROD: That's right.

BRYAN: Well, which?

ROD: Rodrigo in point of fact.

BRYAN: How very classical, how very romantic. Can one be both?

ROD: Surely. My mother.

BRYAN: Is from?

ROD: Was. Paraguay.

BRYAN: More interesting than Edinburgh.

ROD: Not necessarily to Paraguayans.

BRYAN: I suppose not. But to Germans... ja? (*Another damp squib.*) Where the devil has Helier got to?

17

HELIER: (*Enters, dressed.*) Helier's got to right here. How do you do, Mr... Ah...

BRYAN: Leonard.

HELIER: Leonard – how do you do? Has my husband gone so far in the social square dance as to offer you a drink?

ROD: Yes, thank you. And it's Rod.

HELIER: What is?

ROD: My name.

HELIER: Is what?

BRYAN: It's Rod. His name is. His surname is Leonard. Rod.

HELIER: Rod. But that would be an abbreviation. Wouldn't it?

ROD: Not really.

HELIER: Or a reference?

ROD: Nobody's ever complained – of my work.

HELIER: Well, I should think not. Oh, on the subject – Rod – do you know the meaning of... hell, where did I put it?

She hunts for, finds and consults her shorthand pad.

Ah, here. Aphanasis?

ROD: Well, it's probably something to do with invisibility – Aphanes: invisible: Greek. I think.

HELIER: What do you mean, you think? Don't pretend to be dumber than you are – it really irritates me –

pretending to be cleverer is bad enough. Invisible?
Not "loss of desire" or "castration"?

ROD: (*Keeping his balance, sensing something wrong.*) You could
say that by implication.

HELIER: You don't want to make an enemy of me, you
know.

ROD: No.

BRYAN: For sheer sweetness of disposition you can, on
your good days, make Mother Theresa look like the
Empress Wu.

HELIER: I was just suggesting I might be able to be very
useful.

ROD: I hope I can be too.

BRYAN: I'm sure you will be.

HELIER: I think I should have another drink. You sure
you won't?

BRYAN: Good God, Helier, he's said he doesn't drink twice
already don't go on at him. And are you really sure you
want another? Anyway the shaker's empty.

HELIER: Liar! (*Picks up shaker.*) I knew it. (*Pours herself
a drink.*) The truth is seldom told in this house, Mr... Rod.
Perhaps you will be able to do something about that.
Time somebody did.

ROD: People only lie because one expects too much of
them.

HELIER: Or because they expect too much of you,
perhaps? Do you tell the truth... Rod?

ROD: As often as I can.

BRYAN: Isn't that one of those questions whose answer can never be believable? "All Greeks are liars – That is not true – I am Greek" – you know the kind of thing. Beacon Reader One in Logic.

HELIER: But you are not Greek, are you? (*With faintly erotic enphasis.*) Not in *any* way?

ROD: No. That's right.

HELIER: But something?

ROD: Inevitably.

BRYAN: Oh, don't be so stupid. Of course he is something. South American in fact. Well half.

HELIER: And how do South Americans well half rate in Logic – or truth-telling?

ROD: Much like anyone else. Their behaviour is conditioned by idleness.

HELIER: But you are industrious?

BRYAN/ROD: (*Together.*) That's right.

HELIER: Surely that really is a question he could, indeed should answer for himself.

BRYAN: I just meant that a man as busy, as famous as Courtney would hardly have employed him had he not been.

HELIER: Ah, yes, just what did you do for Courtney?

ROD: A little bit of almost everything, I suppose... I went along with his enthusiasms.

HELIER: You'd have had to do a lot for him after his wife died.

ROD: I think I was able to help. In my way.

HELIER: Did you like him?

ROD: The work was often very interesting.

HELIER: (*Sharp.*) I asked whether you liked him.

ROD: People as famous as that you don't really like or dislike them, I find.

HELIER: Do you? I find it polarises one's affections very clearly.

BRYAN: Good old-fashioned feminine point of view.

HELIER: Why does that remark not surprise me?

BRYAN: Because you think it unsophisticated to show surprise. At anything. But enthusiasm need not necessarily be a provincial virtue.

HELIER: (*Joins ROD at the window.*) Do you have enthusiasms, Rod?

ROD: Constantly.

HELIER: What are your current ones?

ROD: In any particular order?

HELIER: Intensity? Vulgarity? Alphabetical?

ROD: Bicycling, Viennese operetta and Manhattans.

HELIER: We *shall* have to mind our Ps and Qs.

BRYAN: I thought you said you didn't drink.

ROD: No, I just said I didn't want a drink at that moment. Before lunch.

Gong.

HELIER: Do you always make things happen like that? I'm starving.

BRYAN: (*Stopping at the door.*) Come along. What is it?

ROD: About the job?

BRYAN: Oh – of course, if you want it, that is.

ROD: Oh, I want it.

BRYAN: Yes, I thought you might.

~

Scene Two

Afternoon. Some days later. BRYAN is sitting in an armchair, watching ROD correcting a set of galley proofs.

BRYAN: (*After a leisurely pause.*) You really are rapidly becoming indispensable.

ROD: Somebody once said that means you must be up to no good.

BRYAN: What's your view on that?

ROD: It's laziness really. I hate having to spend time looking for things, so I keep them in the right places. Lots of people find it rather irritating.

BRYAN: Lots of untidy people.

ROD: Not only them.

BRYAN: Well, you can irritate me as much as you want. How are those galleys?

ROD: I've picked up a few typos, nothing much: oh – and I've made a couple of suggestions in the margin, just where it didn't seem completely clear – to me at any rate. Here for instance.

BRYAN: Yes, that is much clearer. Thank you. I can see I'll be having to look out for you. Comes of doing things in too much of a hurry, I'm afraid. Thank you.

ROD: I'll have them ready to pick up this evening, unless you want to see them first, or will you wait till you can see it in page proof?

BRYAN: Wait till it's in page. The less I have to do with the bloody thing from now on the better. I'd rather read my books than write them, but there are limits.

ROD: Hahaha! Misprint of the week – "When criticising Big Ben, as with much neo-Gothic building, one should remember the claims of other timepieces in public places. Considerations of size should not weigh too heavily in judging the merits of a cock."

BRYAN: Much they know. I've got a quote later on, from Delacroix – "Young men are always more given to admiring what is gigantic than what is reasonable."

ROD: There you are then. The printers are sending a bike for these at five. Though I don't know what all the rush is about.

BRYAN: Mostly about me missing two deadlines, I fear. I really hated this one. Before you arrived, I used to take every opportunity of putting off work on it. Posting letters, walking the dog unnecessarily, turning out cupboards, sewing on buttons – anything. I used to send postcards to people I hadn't seen for ten years, or else I'd seen them the evening before. I mean, all beginnings are bad; every time you sit in front of a blank sheet of paper, you are starting from scratch again – you can't talk of a career. But this was the worst. In recent years anyway.

ROD: Vanity.

BRYAN: What?

ROD: The vanity of being ashamed to give the world anything but the best. But since the best can only come with successive effort, you wait and wait and in the end you can't even produce second-rate work. Modesty can betray just as badly as anything else, and often serves as a cloak for egoism.

BRYAN: I don't know why I let you talk to me like that.

ROD: Don't you?

BRYAN: Yes. Because I want you to. As I said, indispensable.

ROD: But up to no good.

BRYAN: I don't think that matters any more.

ROD: I'm glad you agree.

BRYAN: That's settled then.

ROD: For the time being.

BRYAN: What makes you say that? What other little surprises have you up your sleeve for me? For us? Helier says she can't make you out at all – I suspect that may be because you can make her out perfectly well. All too much so. Mmm?

ROD: (*Deliberately not answering the question.*) What's that strange building in the park out there? Like a little pyramid?

BRYAN: That's the ice-house.

ROD: The what?

BRYAN: The ice-house. Every grand house had one in the eighteenth century and I dare say long before that. You put ice in them in the winter storing it underground, and somehow or other it stayed frozen well into the summer, right through sometimes, I'd guess.

ROD: What was the point of the pyramid?

BRYAN: Pyramids seemed to be the answer to everything then: Science, Reason, Freemasonry. Now we just think they'll sharpen razor blades.

ROD: But where did the ice come from in the first place?

BRYAN: They probably fished it out of the river. Winters were a lot colder in those days, remember. The rivers froze over regularly. Whole oxen roasted on the Thames, that sort of thing.

ROD: Anyway it's a crass enough metaphor of the human condition.

BRYAN: Ice stored up while the spirit freezes over?

ROD: Yes. Then when it's finally needed it's probably all melted away. Can you get into it?

BRYAN: No, it's all locked up now – boarded up. Keep out courting couples. And worse. Vagrants. Children.

ROD: Don't suppose there's anything inside by now. Not even ice. Few puddles maybe.

BRYAN: It's a good death.

ROD: What is?

BRYAN: Dying of cold.

ROD: Ever try it?

BRYAN: Well, no.

ROD: Well, then.

BRYAN: No, but they say, once you stop panicking, you have these visions. Not like drowning, with all your life passing in front of you. More visions of how you think your life should have been – if you'd only known.

ROD: How someone feels at the end of his life is a pretty good indication of what he feels to have been the quality of it all. And what kind of visions would you have?

BRYAN: I have an idea of something Greek – classical – white marble, the shadows of olive trees on the groups of young people listening to the teaching of a philosopher. Platonic.

ROD: The true the beautiful? Usually just an excuse for picking up some more than usually pretty boy.

BRYAN: (*Stiffly.*) Rather more likely to be Helier's vision, I think.

ROD: Do you? Do you have any idea what her visions might really be? A difficult thing predicting the intimate feelings of other people, particularly if we know them well – or think we do. I expect she'd surprise you.

BRYAN: She inflicted her last surprise on me when she married me. Or very shortly afterwards.

ROD: Did you ever have any children?

BRYAN: How about minding your own bloody business?

ROD: Sorry.

Pause.

I suppose ice preserves itself. What happens in igloos? The Eskimos must keep warm in them. Can they light a fire? You only ever see them covered in fur.

BRYAN: Well, I don't suppose they go short of a cube or two for their G & Ts. Dear God, here I am complaining about deadlines, when I should be out harpooning polar bears or whatever.

ROD: Wicked ungrateful girl and the angels will weep for you.

BRYAN: (*Frosty.*) I take it that was a quotation. It had that ring to it. I hope it was, anyway – while on ice, do you

27

want a drink? It's way after lunch, and no one else is going to drink all that American whisky you've imported.

ROD: I must stay sane till I get through these. (*Points to galleys.*) Who knows what errors might creep in? All those young people being led astray by misprints in the teaching of their philosopher. That wasn't always your vision of hypothermia, was it?

BRYAN: No. I imagine at twenty I envisioned an infinite panorama of sexual success. I didn't really think there was any other kind. In fact, I equated the two. Probably because it was the only success I'd had – up to then.

ROD: Done alright since, though, haven't you?

BRYAN: For sex? Or success? One tends to bleed into the other. And neither is ever really the kind you want.

ROD: You can always pay for sex. Do you?

BRYAN: Only emotionally.

ROD: Just as well there's still imagination to fill the gaps.

BRYAN: Quite. Remember, there's always four to a bed – two participants and the two people they are thinking of.

ROD: What happens if they're both thinking of the same person?

BRYAN: Well, that's not very... Then there would be three. I suppose. You never said what your vision of death by ice would be.

ROD: Turmoil. Confusion. Unreason. All the things I try to avoid.

BRYAN: In life?

ROD: Yes.

BRYAN: I never know what you're thinking.

ROD: Thinking?

BRYAN: Yes, for Christ's sake, thinking. Talking to you –
it's like firing a gun into a cushion.

ROD: How would you expect – like me to react?

BRYAN: Like a human being, which I take it you are –
in your heart of hearts, that remote and murky region.

ROD: Oh, yes.

BRYAN: There you go again.

ROD: Sorry. Is it depriving you of success?

BRYAN: In a way.

ROD: Success or its next-of-kin?

BRYAN: What do you... Sex? Well, I don't think...
it hardly seems...

ROD: You said the visions only come when you stop
panicking. So stop. Have a drink.

He mixes one.

BRYAN: No, well maybe... yes.

Rod pours and gives him a drink.

You won't join me? What's stopping you now?
Proofs? Oh, leave them. We can pick up any other
mistakes in page.

ROD: (*Patting the window seat.*) Come and sit with me,
then. Here.

BRYAN: (*Going to another chair.*) There.

ROD: (*Naturally, as if they were together.*) That better?

BRYAN: (*Taking his tone.*) Yes. Much.

ROD: Good.

BRYAN: Now what do you have in mind?

ROD: That's for you to say, I would think. As my
employer, if for no other reason. Certainly as my
philosopher. My Platonic philosopher. What is in
your mind?

BRYAN: Definitely not philosophical – nor Platonic.
I don't suppose I could make a philosophic
impression on you if I tried.

ROD: Not that you have – yet. But something must remain.

BRYAN: Oh, yes, all the architecture. The columns, the
terraces, the steps, the benches, the sunlight and the
olive trees. And the clear sky arching over the whole
scene.

ROD: (*Dismissive.*) Aesthetics. Where are the people?

BRYAN: Yes, I expect the eager boys and girls are still
there.

ROD: Waiting for the philosopher.

BRYAN: (*Slight regret.*) They do not need a philosopher.
They themselves are the answer. To any question they
would think of putting to him. If only they knew it.

ROD: (*Derisive.*) Sentiment. And liberal sentiment at that.
You don't believe it.

BRYAN: (*Defensive.*) I would like to. And I don't think
I'm sentimental.

ROD: Only because you feel guilty about it. Because you're rich enough to do so. It's what keeps people going through the bad times, though. That makes women more sentimental than men.

BRYAN: Try that one on Helier and see where it gets you.

ROD: No, but you.

BRYAN: Oh, I've tried everything by now.

ROD: Except submission.

BRYAN: Oh, that too.

ROD: But the wrong kind. People think they're submitting when all they're doing is giving orders. Submission is not pleasant, though the temptation to find it so is strong in certain persons. And now I think I will yes have a drink.

BRYAN: Good idea. (*Holds out his glass.*) I could do with freshening up a bit.

ROD: (*Identical intonation.*) And now I think I will yes have a drink.

BRYAN: Oh. Yes.

He goes over to the trolley.

ROD: Learning.

BRYAN: What are the proportions?

ROD: Two Bourbon. One French. One Italian. Dash of bitters. (*Sharp.*) Got that?

BRYAN: Of course. (*At shaker.*) Now, let's see. Two Bourbon. Yes. One each vermouth? Dash of bitters. Is that right? Good. There we are. Cherry?

31

ROD: No, I've had one before, thank you.

BRYAN: See how that suits you. Alright? Good. Shall I turn the light on?

ROD: No.

BRYAN: Alright. Good. (*Looking out of the window.*)There's a light in the ice-house. I wonder what that is. Oh, no it's just the end of sunlight.

ROD: Come back here and sit down.

BRYAN goes to his old chair.

BRYAN: Maybe we should get one thing straight...

ROD: Exactly what I was thinking. And I know whose.

BRYAN: (*Rising nervously and going to the bar.*) I must get my drink.

ROD: It will have been some time, no?

BRYAN: What will?

ROD: Oh, come on. Join the party.

BRYAN: What do you mean – party?

ROD: Well I don't mean the Nazi Party. Some time since you indulged yourself in this way.

BRYAN: Way?

ROD: Do stop repeating everything I say. Indulge yourself, by total immersion in your visions from the ice-house: now's your chance, nothing can get in the way now. Come with me where nothing jars. You can hear the waves. You can see the columns, the steps, the olive trees, the young boys and girls drinking in your every word. Isn't that what you wanted? Where

32

even the words are sexy. Boys. Girls. The tongue makes them sound like drinks. Take my hand and follow – here is fulfilment – here is success. Drink it – open yourself to it. Don't disappoint me after such a wait. You've no idea of the disappointment when we think we have power over a body – to be fobbed off with a soul... Drink in the dark, and let the dark drink you.

A silence, broken by BRYAN's voice, lecturing.

BRYAN: "It is a phenomenon, often observed and frequently opened to discussion, that the style of certain artists in old age differs radically, almost unidentifiably, from the work of their youth and maturity. A sketchiness of technique, as if the artist, taking cognisance, perhaps, of his failing physical powers, could no longer devote his time away from what he wishes to express, is made up for by a deepening of the vision, an attempt to substitute a totality of expression for the mere accumulation of detail, however fascinating. These works are frequently not only filled with a movingly elegiac quality, understandably absent from youthful treatments of similar material, but they also throw a lance into the future, to be picked up by generations to come, of whom the artist can know nothing." Oh! They applauded me. Did they understand it all, I wonder? How could they – they are so young – only children, after all. And yet they seem to know so much.

(*ROD applauds slowly.*) There's something else here. Something I don't know and don't trust. The children have sensed it too. Something is going wrong. The boy there – the one who smiled at me – a messenger of the Gods, do you suppose? – leaning back against an olive tree.

ROD: Waiting for something?

BRYAN: I don't know. The branches of the tree are moving, but there is no wind to stir them. An old woman is approaching him with a bowl in her hand. Begging probably. I've a feeling something has gone badly wrong. There isn't a sound from the others – they're still playing, or dancing, is it? The sky isn't as blue as it was. "Why don't you have any music to dance to?" They don't turn round. Can they not hear me?

ROD: Look at the tree. And the boy. And the old woman. Look!

BRYAN: Something's odd with the tree. The branches are still moving. They're moving round the boy. And the old woman is getting nearer to him. She has a knife with her. She's – oh, oh, oh – she's cutting – yes – cutting his throat – her hands are round him. The tree branches hold him fast. She's licking his throat, drinking the blood of him. Aaaah!

Doorbell – repeated, as BRYAN's climax subsides.

ROD: That'll be the printers for those proofs. Don't go away now.

He goes out with the proofs. Fade out.

~

Scene Three

*Afternoon, a few days later. HELIER sitting in chair where
BRYAN sat before. With a drink. ROD enters, not seeing
her, and goes out to the bedrooms, returning soon, carrying
a Polaroid camera.*

HELIER: Making out?

ROD: Oh! You startled me. I had no idea you were
back. I was told you had gone into town.

HELIER: Inquiring for me, were you?

ROD: No, it was just some letters came for you in the
morning mail – second delivery.

Gives her them.

HELIER: Anything interesting?

ROD: Not to judge from the outside.

HELIER: Still, it's what gets inside that counts, right?

ROD: Right. (*He goes out again.*)

HELIER: You can sweep a girl back on her feet quick
enough, can't you?

(*Pause.*) Round Two. Seconds out of the ring.

Pings her glass.

ROD: (*Re-entering.*) Do you see things between us like
that? A boxing match?

HELIER: No, but I expect you quite enjoy a little
sparring before getting down to things, *oui ou non*?

ROD: With the right person.

HELIER: And that isn't me?

ROD: The perspective can change quite suddenly sometimes.

HELIER: That would depend very much where you were sitting. Fill my glass.

ROD: (*A whiff of the Old South.*) Yaz'm. Right privileged to oblahge yew. (*Ordinary voice.*) You really should try the delights of the Manhattan some day.

HELIER: I'm sure I should. And doubtless shall. All in good time. Is that Bryan's Polaroid?

ROD: Yes. It needs a new film.

HELIER: What's he been using it for?

ROD: I imagine taking photographs.

HELIER: Fancy.

ROD: There's one picture left. Shall I?

HELIER: Or shall I?

ROD: Well, one of us had better yield to the temptation, or the whole thing becomes ridiculous.

HELIER: It should have one of those delayed action things.

ROD: Well it hasn't. Someone has to hold it. So – frown, or puke, or something. (*Flash.*) There.

HELIER: I don't think Bryan can really make you out.

ROD: That's what he thinks about you.

HELIER: Well, I won't say you're a perfect crystal, the very openest of books, but I think, yes, I think I do have one or two minor insights.

ROD: Into?

HELIER: What makes you tick.

ROD: And what does?

HELIER: Like any good watch. Being wound up.

ROD: And you're the woman to do it?

HELIER: I think we can produce a few good results.
    In a fair fight.

ROD: It's all got to be combat with you, hasn't it?

HELIER: Well, I mean, you ever watch it going on?

ROD: (*Changing tack.*) Anything in the mail needs dealing with?

HELIER: No, just bills. Pay them.

ROD: Why, I'd be right glad to, ma'am.

HELIER: Don't get cute with me. I told you not to make me
    an enemy the day you came here.

ROD: But you don't like friends very much, do you?

HELIER: Not unless they're just to talk to. No, I don't. Do
    you have friends?

ROD: Sometimes.

HELIER: You're welcome to ask them here, you know.

ROD: I don't think so.

HELIER: I just wondered if there hadn't been someone quite
    recently, and you might have been shy about saying.
    Someone here.

ROD: What makes you think that?

HELIER: Oh, things one notices. In the bathroom and such.
    Kitchen. I know it's a cliché, but women really do notice
    these things. Towels askew and... well, things.

37

ROD: I answered the phone in your bedroom the other day – I was passing as it rang – and then I did have a pee in your bathroom, and used the soap. I think that's the full extent of the barbarian invasion.

HELIER: I told you, you're really welcome.

ROD: Another thing you told me – the day I came here – was that no one ever told the truth in this house. Do you still think that?

HELIER: If anyone's belief should have solidified it's yours. What do you think?

ROD: I find they will if cornered.

HELIER: Are you trying to corner me?

ROD: I certainly hope you will tell me the truth.

HELIER: What about?

ROD: The things you imagine for a start. That should be painless – no one can check your facts. (*At the window.*) It gets dark very early now – hardly six and you can't see across the park properly. That looks like smoke coming out of the ice-house... what could it be? No, it's a bonfire behind it – there's the park-keeper.

HELIER: I hate it when the clocks go back. Suddenly the darkness is just there all at once. Brr!

ROD: All that ice just sitting underground – waiting to melt. That's all ice does, it's not interesting in any condition except dissolution.

HELIER: It's all waiting to be taken up in one mighty Martini. Please.

Proffers glass.

ROD: Not Manhattan?

HELIER: Not yet. Its time will come. For you it has already.
It's after six by now surely.

ROD: Near enough.

HELIER: Well there you are then.

ROD: (*Handing her glass.*) There you are.

HELIER: What's the picture come out like?

ROD: Not a success. I'm no good at them. (*Throwing
it to her.*)

HELIER: Dear God, I look like The Wreck of the Hesperus.

ROD: You're lucky I got your head in at all.

HELIER: What the hell's happened to Bryan? As if
I cared.

ROD: He's got a meeting with the people from...

HELIER: I said "as if I cared". I don't want to know
what lie he told you about where he was going.

ROD: No, it wasn't a lie. They made the appointment some
days ago, and rang up this morning to confirm.

HELIER: I don't think anything actually happens in these
assignments. Not unless something has gone dangerously
adrift with his metabolism that I don't know about. People
can be so secretive sometimes, *nicht wahr*?

ROD: I used to make a charge every time I made love
to someone.

HELIER: Used to?

ROD: Oh, yes. I would insist they tell me something
about themselves they had never told anyone else.

HELIER: With interesting results?

ROD: Sometimes very. One person told me she had or had had cancer. One told me about inheriting half a million pounds from a lover. Another had robbed her dying mother of half a fortune. One described boys being disembowelled on the steps of a Greek temple by old women who drank their blood.

HELIER makes a noise of faint but marked distaste.

I think everything that happens to anyone is told to someone. Does it matter to whom?

HELIER: It would be nice to think it was the person they were living with.

ROD: At the time.

HELIER: Very well. At the time. Bryan thinks it all goes into his writing. But it doesn't really. You always feel something held back. Do you think he is a good writer?

ROD: (*Taking care.*) He is certainly a very accomplished one.

HELIER: That's like saying he's a very useful actor or she doesn't sweat much for a fat girl. It indicates individuality without personality. Hell, if he isn't accomplished, why's his passport say "Occupation Writer"?

ROD: Information on passports is often misleading, not just the photograph. The trouble starts when two exclusive confidences collide, when someone imposes a fantasy on what is already someone else's fantasy. Always means trouble. The purity of the more yielding wish is corrupted by the stronger.

HELIER: Are you saying keep your fantasies to yourself?

ROD: No, I'm saying don't impose them on other people, particularly if you're sleeping with them at the time. All addicts are in love with secrecy.

HELIER: I don't have fantasies. Women don't need them.

ROD: Well that's got to be a lie to start with. What do they use instead?

HELIER: Things that happen to them.

ROD: In other words fantasies based on fact – like any other.

HELIER: You know how I met Bryan? It was in Bristol. Outside a cinema. A lorry had just knocked into a pigeon – yes, I know it sounds ridiculous, but there it was, fluttering away on its one remaining wing, and oh, going round and round, pivoting on its head. Clearly in no fit condition. I had screamed "Bastard" at the lorry-driver, who had replied "They're just vermin, darlin'" and driven off. Bryan came up, looked at the bird and said "I suppose one ought to put it out of its misery" and, in a rare moment of physical decisiveness, stamped on its head. Some freakish effect of pressure, no doubt, had alas to dictate that the bird's blood should spurt up and get all over the bottom of my dress – pale pink, not a colour I've been able to wear since – and I just stood there, looking like Jackie Kennedy at LBJ's swearing-in. I didn't have hysterics or anything, but it made me unnaturally talkative and next thing I was in a hotel room telling him the story of my life.

ROD: Did he tell you the story of his?

HELIER: Not then, and not that much since, but we became inseparable, and marriage seemed the only possible end of such a relationship. And of course, that's what it was – the end of it. We're not exactly a matching set, but we get along. I need another drink. (*Hands over her glass.*)

ROD: What will you have?

HELIER: A hangover, I don't doubt. What I usually have, of course. Are there other drinks?

ROD: Manhattans?

HELIER: I've acted quite enough out of character for the time being.

ROD: Telling me this? It's what I charge. I told you. It is the first time you've told anyone else?

HELIER: Oh, yes. Straight from the horse's brain. (*He hands her her drink.*) Thank you. You also said, if I remember, that it was a charge you made for making love to someone. Is that what you think you're doing?

ROD: Keep going. You want me to turn the light on?

HELIER: No. Yes. Whatever.

ROD: Can I quote you on that?

HELIER: Not on that; not on anything else, if you value your … well, don't.

ROD: (*Taking advantage of her confusion.*) Now tell me about the child.

HELIER: Child? What are you talking about?

ROD: Your child.

HELIER: I don't know what you mean. What child?

ROD: Your child.

HELIER: I never had a child. You shouldn't talk to me like – about – like that.

ROD: Drink your drink.

HELIER: Oh, yes, and then you pour me another and then another until I'll admit to anything you throw at me. You don't have to be a genius to see that.

ROD: It's an advantage, though, if you want to be sure.

HELIER: What did Bryan tell you?

ROD: Told me to mind my own business.

HELIER: And you don't?

ROD: As you see. Now tell me.

HELIER: Get him to.

ROD: Nothing doing there.

HELIER: Nor here.

ROD: One advantage of telling the truth is that you don't have to remember what lies you told.

HELIER: The same advantage could come from keeping your mouth shut.

ROD: But you won't do that – because you don't want to. And don't look offended. That really doesn't suit the over-thirties.

HELIER: Well, I think I *am* offended.

ROD: Offending people is a bit like invading Russia. It's amazing how far you can get before you meet disaster.

HELIER: But that is hardly the point, is it? The problem is to get more than halfway; in other words, do you have a return ticket?

ROD: In this household you need a season.

HELIER: You know, if you want to get to the top as a sex-on-a-stick seducer it's no use just having cult appeal – you have to appeal to the majority. And that means not overdoing anything that might make it look like competition, like – how shall I put this... intelligence. Nobody loves a smart ass, but they'll roll over and lick Marmite off his cock in comparison with someone who makes them feel they might be being a touch slow on the uptake. And as women always think that somehow the joke is on them, you see what I mean... I hope?

ROD: That doesn't sound like the speech of a stupid woman.

HELIER: I didn't say it was. I was just giving you a bit of advice. Not a very popular move, I dare say.

ROD: No, I'm not so besotted with my own capacities as to turn down something to my advantage.

HELIER: I hardly supposed so. Do you know where Bryan is this afternoon? He confides in you chiefly these days.

ROD: Last time you asked you said you didn't care. Do you want me to tell you?

HELIER: I can see you're with child to do so, so do so.

ROD: He's gone to Titania Books to see his editor. The new book's out next week and they wanted to talk over some bits and pieces, and I think, give him a contract for another.

HELIER: So you see, Helier, he is a success after all. Why yes, Rod, I always knew he would be if only he could find the right person to hold his hand. Well, Helier, I hope I've been a little help to him in my own small way. Oh, you have, Rod, you have indeed. Are you sure that's where he's gone? He's staying pretty late for a business appointment. Or disappointment, perhaps. In which case, he may just have ejected Teddy from the pram.

ROD: Probably stayed on for a drink with the boss. Free champagne. You know the way.

HELIER: Well, he does.

ROD: He'll be back for dinner. What's that bell for?

HELIER: Just the park closing. Dusk. Gloaming. The fall of night. *Goetter dammer...* whatnot – whatever. You should know that by now.

ROD: Sure. Bonfire still going merrily, I perceive.

HELIER: Crackle, crackle, crackle.

They clink glasses. Fade out.

~

Scene Four

A few days later. Late afternoon. ROD reading page proofs.
Enter BRYAN with newspaper from outside.

ROD: Well, they came eventually. The final page proofs.
Now we have to turn them round in twenty-four hours
flat. After that they won't guarantee to make changes.
They're getting out an advance copy tonight, ready
for us tomorrow. But no more than twenty-four hours
– they were clear on that.

BRYAN: Can we do that?

ROD: Oh, sure.

BRYAN: (*None too good-naturedly.*) Better get on with it
then, hadn't we?

ROD: I was concentrating on the bit you skipped in the
galleys. Seems all right.

BRYAN: Told you so.

ROD: Yes.

BRYAN: Well, you don't have to check it twice. Or are
you trying to create work for yourself? If you've
nothing better to do you'd better read that.

(*Throws him the paper and goes to the door.*) Helier!

HELIER: (*Off.*) What?

BRYAN: Here a minute. (*Takes off overcoat and scarf.*
To ROD.) What about that, then?

ROD: It must have been a good month ago by now.
What took them so long?

HELIER: What is it?

BRYAN: Courtney was found dead. In his flat. Here.

HELIER: (*Reads.*) "Police entering the Harley Street flat
of Sir Courtney Newnham this morning found the
body of the eminent former Government advisor, who
had apparently died of an overdose of barbiturates. Sir
Courtney (74) whose wife died earlier this year, had for
some time been suffering from a heart condition
etcetera etcetera ..." Oh, how dreadful, poor Courtney,
lying there a whole month, I'm so sorry.

BRYAN: Had he been depressed lately, do you think?

HELIER: We'd seen so little of him since Marjorie died.
We really ought to have made more of an...

BRYAN: He'd have relied on you a lot, Rodrigo, after his
wife died. You would have had to make up for a lot of
things she did for him, I suppose.

HELIER: How do people get hold of things like
overdoses, for Heaven's sake? I mean, where
would one go for...

ROD: He had a repeating prescription. He probably
saved up pills till he had enough, just in case he felt
he needed them.

BRYAN: Yes, for God's sake, I should think most
households have enough poison in them somewhere
or other to massacre the inhabitants twice over. I'm
sure this one does.

HELIER: Really, like what?

BRYAN: Oh, come on, Helier, you know the state of the
bathroom cupboard. I don't suppose it's much worse
than ninety per cent of the bathroom cupboards
through the length and breadth of the Greater British
Reich, but I'm quite sure we could lay the three of us

47

pretty flat in less time than it takes to tell, or absorb anyway. Did you know about his prescription?

ROD: Certainly. He asked me to get it filled several times.

BRYAN: So you knew how much he was taking?

ROD: I knew how much I was buying.

BRYAN: But you knew nothing of what happened to it after that?

ROD: No, I didn't.

BRYAN: When did he write you that reference?

ROD: Just before I came here. I think. Why?

BRYAN: The signature looked a little shaky, that's all.

ROD: Well, it probably would. He was not well. It was after his stroke. What are all these questions, anyway? Anyone would think...

BRYAN: Yes?

ROD: Well, that you were the police or something.

BRYAN: Why should the police be at all interested? It says in the paper they're treating the death as natural. Of course, that's just what the paper says.

ROD: I'd better hang your coat up. It'll crease.

He takes it out.

BRYAN: He gets odder, you know.

HELIER: Oh, please, next thing you'll be saying he murdered Courtney. Leave it alone, and Rod too while you're at it. Are you going off him, now the book's as good as ready?

BRYAN: "Going off him" is hardly the phrase I'd
have chosen myself. But – yes – his usefulness is
diminishing. What was his phrase when he first
came here? "I became unnecessary", I think. Well,
he's becoming just that. I can't use full-time secretaries
– can't think of enough things for them to do.

HELIER: Did you ever pick up on that reference?

BRYAN: You mean, check back with Courtney?

HELIER: Yes.

BRYAN: I did ring him once, but there was no answer,
and later on it didn't seem...

HELIER: No, I don't suppose... Too late now anyway.

ROD: (*Re-entering.*) Oh, I forgot to ask. Did Titania offer
you another contract?

BRYAN: Yes, indeed they did and it sounds a very well-
cushioned one at that. It's in my coat pocket.

ROD: Oh, let me get it.

BRYAN: No, you sit down. I want you to cast an eye
over it, tell me what you think. (*Out.*)

HELIER: He's being a bit neurotic today. I think he
was very fond of Courtney.

ROD: As he of him.

HELIER: Otherwise he would hardly have given you
such a glowing reference, would he?

ROD: What? Oh, no. I suppose not.

BRYAN: (*Back in.*) Just take a peek at this one – will it
make us rich?

HELIER: A book on aesthetics? – come off it.

BRYAN: No, but it's part of a whole projected series.

Takes an envelope out of the pocket. A sheaf of Polaroid photos flutters to the floor.

What's that?

ROD: (*Not moving.*) Here, let me.

But HELIER is there first.

HELIER: Hang on a minute. What are these? (*Looking at them.*) For Christ's sake, Bryan, just what have you been getting up to?

BRYAN: I don't know where they came from.

HELIER: Am I really supposed to believe that? For God's sake, Rod, this is you!

BRYAN: Let me see that. What the hell is this?

ROD: Well, Bryan, you must surely remember...

HELIER: And in my bedroom. Bryan, I don't believe this.

BRYAN: But I didn't take these. I wasn't there.

HELIER: Pictures have to be taken by someone. Someone has to be there. There has to be someone.

BRYAN: (*To ROD.*) I knew you were up to no good. I said so.

ROD: I remember. I told you to be careful. Not to carry them around. Keep them somewhere safe.

HELIER: You mean this was a conspiracy?

BRYAN: NO!!

ROD: That's not what I would call it. It was a means of saving you embarrassment.

HELIER: And it's worked a treat, hasn't it?

BRYAN: None of this is what you think.

HELIER: You knowing exactly what I think, of course.

BRYAN: But they aren't pictures of me!

HELIER: Someone had to hold the camera or could
you not find someone to do it for you, like Japanese
tourists do in London? And why would you have
wanted pictures of *yourself*? If my memory is any good,
you would have tried to edit yourself out of them. Of
course, things may have changed, but...

BRYAN: No they have not changed... I mean...

HELIER: Yes, what do you mean? (*Another photograph.*)
What the hell is this one? The man has a mask on.

BRYAN: (*To ROD.*) I shall kill you for this. I promise you,
whatever else I do, I shall kill you.

ROD: That's not what you said before. Not to me,
anyway.

HELIER: No this one isn't even Rod. He may be masked
but there are other differences. I was right though –
it's not an abbreviation – not by a long chalk. This is
another room too.

BRYAN: So it can't be me.

HELIER: Don't be so stupid. Is that your briefcase by
the bed, or not? And what about the scarf? I gave
you that for your last birthday. Look at it! Look at
the damn thing!

(*She picks up his scarf from a chair.*) The last present
you'll get from me, I can assure you. (*Another
photograph.*) Here's the same room again, and the
same man, and another one, I can't make out his face.

BRYAN: Well it can't be me.

HELIER: Not unless you've changed your pigmentation overnight. But the scarf hasn't changed any. (*Another photograph.*) Oh, Rod again, it's almost a relief to see a familiar face. Though I'll tell you one thing – that sofa goes straight into the sale-room Monday morning.

BRYAN: Whatever you say, Helier.

HELIER: (*Another photograph.*) What's all that mess? Is that blood? What have you been doing? That person looks dead. Why is he tied up like that? Oh, you stupid, stupid, stupid man!

BRYAN: It's a fake, it must be a fake.

HELIER: I'll tell you what's a fake, and that is you. (*To ROD.*) Here – YOU! – you were the one said you made a charge for making love – well, if love is what you call this – horror – I don't suppose you cashed in on it yet, so here's my down payment, and you can bet no one's been told it before, or not by me.

BRYAN: What do you mean, Helier?

ROD: You don't have to do this you know.

HELIER: Then see it as a voluntary contribution. Into the sinking fund. In the sunny far-off days before he started opening up his horizons and anticipating the hunting season, Bryan was quite an uxorious little fellow. Not Henry the Eighth you understand but in his way... well anyhow sooner or later his efforts were rewarded, if that's the word I want, and I seemed to be pregnant. I say 'seemed', which may sound odd – I mean one is either pregnant or not – however bear with me – bear with me, oh hahaha, that is really too... The point is that after what seemed an age, it all turns out to be a dermoid cyst the size of a melon –

Ogen for the record, I don't mean some great
honeydew, for Christ's sake, or – what were you
waiting for, a cantaloupe?

BRYAN: Helier, please...

HELIER: Let's hear it from the proud father.

BRYAN: Please don't, Helier. I never said a word; not
to anyone. We agreed... Now this blackmailing little
shit has to be the first...

HELIER: Sticks and stones may break his bones, but for
lasting effect I'd advise cement. Anyway he hasn't
heard the richest bit. Not only, Rodrigo, was the
aforesaid bag of God knows what weighing in at a
pretty healthy tonnage, but it was also equipped with
quite a fistful of long black hair, some skin, not much
but some, along with a fingernail or two and – wait
for it – teeth! I thought: any more and it'll have to
have a name. Put it down for Eton, you know the
kind of thing. Huh?

Silence.

Alone at last!

Prolonged silence.

BRYAN: I feel sick.

HELIER: Oh, you decided to live after all?

ROD: Maybe I'd better go to my room...

BRYAN: I expect you'll have some packing to do –
(*Points to photographs.*) and take those fucking things
with you. You'd better go in the morning. I don't think
I want to see you again.

(*After ROD has left.*) They say that in cities, we are, by
and large, seldom more than ten feet away from a

brown rat. I knew he was up to no good. I told him so. He always denied it.

HELIER: The eminent professor of aesthetics with his legs in the air. How aesthetic can that be? Supple, though, I grant you. Heels over head in love.

BRYAN: Oh, don't. Not any more! I can't take it.

HELIER: I wonder if you know what you've taken already.

BRYAN: I've taken nothing. I don't know how he made those pictures but I swear to you...

HELIER: Oh, don't. Don't bother. You did, you didn't. They were, they weren't. Can it matter any longer? We aren't Romeo and Juliet any more. Is this how they would have ended up, d'you think? Romeo balding and overweight, obsessed with his bowels, imposing his bulk on bored Juliet lookalikes, probably for ready money, in some wretched rented room – rented by which of them? And Juliet, growing more witchlike by the day, drinking too much – yes – (*Holds out her glass.*) please – and beginning not to care what she looks like. Forget the fat and go to a good dressmaker.

BRYAN: It needn't happen like that.

HELIER: Don't start being romantic. Look where it gets you. Got you.

BRYAN: You call that romantic?

HELIER: Some of it, inevitably. Romance is only another word for lies, after all.

BRYAN: What the dictionary calls "an infusion of fiction".

HELIER: They don't know the half of it.

BRYAN: Considering most of the world lives by fiction, don't knock it. Particularly to a writer. You need it as much as any of us. (*Hands her her drink.*)

HELIER: Men need the fantasies more than women – it compensates for their feelings of inadequacy. And after a time, even their fantasies become inadequate. But I don't need to tell you that.

BRYAN: No, my fantasies were quite different – all classical temples and marble and philosophical teachings. Until he muddied the water with images of blood and destruction and everything I had built my life against. Though of course, some of it was accurate. I could kill him for that alone.

HELIER: Then do so.

BRYAN: Do what?

HELIER: Kill him.

BRYAN: Don't be ridiculous.

HELIER: The first decent fantasy I have and he tells me not to be ridiculous.

BRYAN: Well, if it's a fantasy, no reason you shouldn't indulge.

HELIER: I can't do it alone.

BRYAN: All I can offer is Greek temples, and marble and a gathering of talented and beautiful young people listening to the addresses of a philosopher.

HELIER: Was that you?

BRYAN: Was what me?

HELIER: Something he said. Doesn't matter.

BRYAN: And they begin to dance together, though I cannot hear the music, I have no ear for it. Now one of them leaves the flock and makes for the steps of the temple. A springy walk, as if anticipating something, and his dark eyes flick here and there, watchful. Into the olive grove. Back leaning against a tree, hands on hips, thumbs back, fingers forward, waiting, waiting. From the Temple where the doors are opening, comes the old woman with the begging bowl towards him. But the tree is growing, its branches are stretching out and holding him. The sky has clouded over.

HELIER: Is something wrong?

BRYAN: There are no rights and wrongs here. Only what happens. Relax. Sit back with me here.

They are sitting in different chairs, like BRYAN and ROD in scene Two.

I will protect you.

HELIER: From what?

BRYAN: From whatever wishes you harm.

HELIER: Why should anyone wish me that?

BRYAN: There is always something.

HELIER: Tell me what happens.

BRYAN: Watch the boy. Watch the tree. Watch the woman. What's in her hands?

HELIER: The bowl, but she isn't begging. There is something wrong.

BRYAN: What else?

HELIER: A knife. Is it for him? It must be for him. He isn't moving. He can't move. The tree has him too fast. Is the knife for him?

BRYAN: You can make it happen.

HELIER: Yes – into his chest! His heart – rip it out of him. Bury your face in him, in the heart, in the blood – it takes so little – and he is gone. But I am still here. The old woman has gone. But I am here still. The tree has gone. But still... here I am.

BRYAN: Shall I turn the light on?

HELIER: No.

BRYAN: He has brought us together. Guilt will bind us faster than ever love could.

HELIER: You're good. Really good. Guilt through and through. I mean, love's all very well, but for real tenacity give me guilt every time.

BRYAN: Quick-drying cement for the wicked.

HELIER: The normal.

BRYAN: The ordinary.

HELIER: The boring.

BRYAN: Us.

HELIER: You know where the poison is. You were the one who said.

BRYAN: Yes.

HELIER: (*Rises and goes to bedroom door.*) Arrange things. (*Fire-engine bell ringing outside.*) What do you suppose that is?

BRYAN: (*Looking out of the window.*) It's the ice-house. On fire. A merry blaze. And a listed building to boot. How did that start, I wonder?

HELIER: Kids.

~

Scene Five

Doorbell – repeated.

Enter ROD from bedrooms in skin-tight, luridly coloured, lycra cycling vest and shorts. Radio plays Strauss.

ROD goes out to hall.

Enter BRYAN from bedroom, picks up new Martini bottle from trolley and goes back to bedroom. He exits just as ROD is coming back in with envelope, which he opens and extracts an advance copy of BRYAN's book.

He crumples up the wrappings and exits with BRYAN's scarf and overcoat as HELIER comes in from bedroom, looks at the book and goes out to hall, colliding with ROD in the doorway. They do not speak but slide round each other.

ROD goes through to the other door, in which he collides with BRYAN entering. Same thing happens, no words, no contact.

BRYAN has other Martini bottle which he puts on trolley, and takes shaker to kitchen.

HELIER enters from kitchen with cup of coffee, and book, which she puts down on the table, and goes out to the bedroom.

BRYAN comes in from kitchen, replaces shaker on trolley, picks up book and dirty glasses, and starts reading on his way back out to kitchen.

ROD enters from bedrooms, with backpack. He takes Polaroid camera and photographs the room, and the view out of the window, where the ice-house is.

Simultaneous entry of BRYAN and HELIER. ROD swings round to photograph HELIER.

BRYAN lunges forwards and snatches the camera out of his hands. He switches off the radio.

BRYAN: Quite enough trouble with that for one lifetime, thank you. (*Looking at ROD's clothes.*) Festive?

ROD: Cycling.

BRYAN: Of course.

ROD: I told you.

BRYAN: Far?

ROD: Enough.

HELIER: Can't be.

ROD: Oh, yes.

BRYAN: Perhaps.

ROD: Book's nice.

BRYAN: Yes. Thank you.

ROD: Please.

BRYAN: No. Really.

ROD: All right.

BRYAN: When you off?

ROD: Now, sort of.

BRYAN: Address?

ROD: Not yet.

BRYAN: Well, when?

ROD: Let you know.

BRYAN: Right.

ROD: Soon as I.

BRYAN: Of course.

ROD: Won't be long.

BRYAN: I'm sure of that.

ROD: Might as well...

BRYAN: Have a drink first.

ROD: No, I...

BRYAN: Oh, come, no hard...

ROD: No, none.

HELIER: Have you both taken a vow of something? You
    sound as if you were sending telegrams to each other.
    If the man wants a drink give him one, if he doesn't
    that's that then. Just give me one.

BRYAN: I think we should swap drinks as it's the end...
    well, today. You, Rodrigo, will know the flower of
    civilisation otherwise known as a dry Martini, and
    we shall finally know the delights of the Manhattan.

HELIER: Oh, I couldn't contemplate such a departure.

BRYAN: (*To ROD.*) And you shall mix them – the
    practised hand.

HELIER: I'll say.

ROD: Original or Modern?

BRYAN: Is that a difference of style or content?

ROD: Original with Italian, Modern with French.

HELIER: Oh, French, for Heaven's sake, not that sticky sweet muck.

BRYAN: No, no, Original is how things should be. (*Significantly.*) Believe me, Helier.

HELIER: Oh, alright, just get it over with.

BRYAN: Ice? Where?

HELIER: Where it always is. (*BRYAN goes off to get it.*) Do you really need – want a drink at this hour?

BRYAN: Of course. We all do. It's a cele… an occasion. Now for the Martini of your dreams. (*Mixing it, using Vermouth from the new bottle, leaving the cap off.*) Have you really never had one before?

ROD: Oddly, no.

BRYAN: Where on earth did you go to school?

ROD: Universidad Católica de Asunción.

BRYAN: There we are then. Try that. I might have been a little heavy on the vermouth. "Wormwood, wormwood" – Hamlet somewhere or other.

HELIER: Oh, this is quite nice – like nursery cough mixture.

ROD: (*Downs it in one – like vodka.*) How many of these do those American businessmen drink – and before lunch? I shall hardly dare get on a bike.

BRYAN: It's an important stage in a boy's life – like the Tour de France.

ROD: I'll be lucky if I can stay in the saddle, never mind about pedalling. No, really no more, I think, well, thank you.

BRYAN refills his glass.

BRYAN: No, it's for me to thank you. I do have to admit I would never have finished the book without your help.

ROD: Well, I hope it's a great success, despite everything.

HELIER: Really?

ROD: Yessss... it deserves to be. It's very accomplished.

HELIER: Aaah, yes.

ROD: Don't suppose there's any chance of a reference?

BRYAN: That should hardly worry a man of your talents.

ROD: (*Draining his glass.*) Well goodbye, then.

BRYAN: I'll see you out.

ROD: Escort me off the premises?

BRYAN: More or less.

ROD: (*Swaying slightly.*) 'I should have never switched to Martinis.' (*Blank looks from the other two.*) Humphrey Bogart? Famous last words.

BRYAN gives a loud clattering laugh and goes out. ROD follows him.

HELIER: (*Alone.*) Right. Time for a real drink. High time.

Mixes a Martini, and one for BRYAN, who re-enters.

There: for a Good Boy.

BRYAN takes glass.

BRYAN: Cheers, Rod!

HELIER: Cheers, Rod!

They clink glasses.

BRYAN: Shouldn't think he'll make it to the bridge.

HELIER: He can have a nice lie down in the ice-house. What's left of it.

BRYAN: (*At the window.*) Just let him get clear of the house. Once he's past the park gates, no one'll know anything of him. No, there isn't much left of it, you're right, the roof is quite gone, fallen in. Just a heap of charred rafters and rubble: poor old ice-house. Pray God they don't do anything daft and goody-goody like restoring it. Such a fitting end – for it, that is: (*Sketches a headline.*) English Heritage Building blitzed in Fire Horror. Well, that's done! Cheers! (*Back to drinks trolley for another.*) By the way, which Martini did you use? (*Picks up both new and old Martini bottles, now identical in appearance, and looks at them with mounting apprehension. The door buzzer sounds insistently.*) Oh, dear God!

Blackout.

End.